My First Book about the Animal Alphabet

Amazing Animal Books
Children's Picture Books

By Molly Davidson

Mendon Cottage Books

JD-Biz Publishing

Read More Amazing Animal Books

Purchase at Amazon.com

Download Free Books!
http://MendonCottageBooks.com

 is for an alligator.

![alligator photograph]

They can be 11 feet long and weigh up to 1,000 pounds.

B is for a bumble bee.

The buzzing sound they make is actually their wings; they flap over 200 times per second!

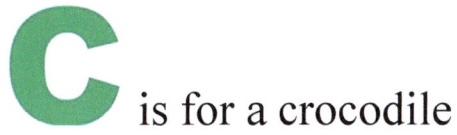 is for a crocodile

A crocodile is different from an alligator because their mouth is a V- shape instead of a U - shape.

D is for a dog.

There are over 340 different breeds of dogs all over the World.

Dogs are the third most popular pet, behind fish and cats.

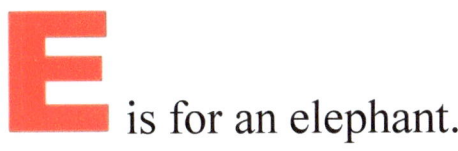 is for an elephant.

The elephant is the heaviest animal on land.

It weighs up to 6 tons (12,000 pounds), that is almost the weight of a school bus!

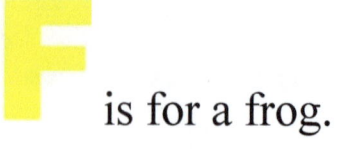 is for a frog.

A frog will shed its skin about once a week, and will usually eat it.

 is for goat.

Goats' eyes are rectangular, not round; this is how they are able to see at night.

Some goats can climb trees and a few can jump as high as 5 feet.

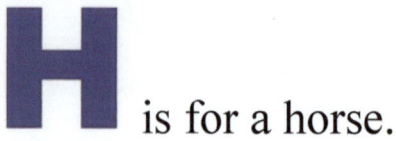 is for a horse.

Horses can sleep standing up and lying down.

A horse's eyes are on the side of his head, this means he can see almost in every direction, without moving his head.

I is for an iguana.

Iguanas are cold blooded, so they have to live where it is warm and sunny, so they can keep themselves warm and alive.

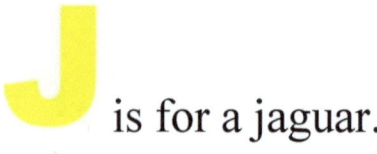
J is for a jaguar.

Jaguars usually hunt on the ground, but sometimes they will pounce from up in a tree.

Most of the time they kill their prey will one bite, crushing its skull.

 is for a kangaroo.

A baby kangaroo is called a joey. Is it only about the size of a lima bean when it is born.

L is for a lion.

A lion's roar can be heard as far as 5 miles away.

The girls do most of the hunting; they hunt at night, and most of the time in groups.

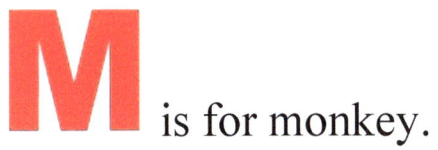 is for monkey.

A group of monkeys is known as a tribe, troop, or mission.

There are 264 different species of monkeys in the World.

 is for a newt.

Newts can make any new body parts.

If they lose their tail, they will grow a new one.

If they get their eye poked out, they will grow a new one.

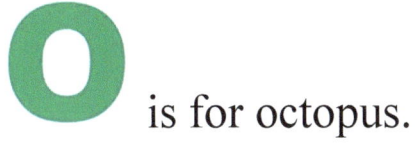 is for octopus.

Octopus are very smart, they can remove a plug and unscrew a container in order to get prey out.

P is for penguin.

Penguins spend 3 out of 4 hours in the water.

Penguins live in one of the coldest climates; it can get down to -40°F, with wind speeds of 89 miles per hour.

 is for a quail.

Quails can mate and lay eggs when they are only 2 months old.

They can lay up to 12 eggs at one time.

R is for rattlesnake.

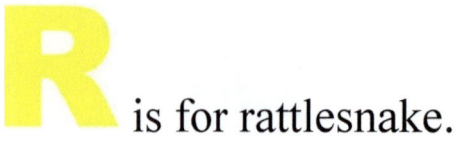

Rattlesnakes can be any length from about 1 to 8 feet.

Humans that are bit by rattlesnakes rarely die; they usually can get medical help fast enough.

 is for seal.

A seal can eat up to 10 pounds of fish in one day.

Baby seals are in their mother for 10 months before they are born.

T is for turtle.

Turtles have been on the earth since the dinosaurs.

Turtles, on average, live about 80 years.

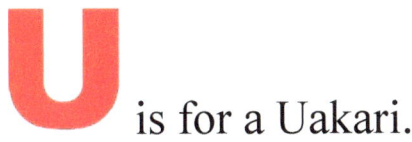 is for a Uakari.

Evgenia Kononova © <u>Wikimedia Commons</u>

These bald, red faced monkeys only live in the Amazon Rain Forest.

 is for vulture.

Vultures have super good eyesight.

They can spot a 3 foot animal carcass from up to 4 miles away.

 is for a whale.

The blue whale is the largest animal to ever live on the earth; it is even bigger than the dinosaurs.

A whale's heart is the size of a VW bug car, and weighs 990 pounds.

 is for xenus.

![Two ground squirrels standing upright on sandy ground]

Hans Hillewaert © <u>Wikimedia Commons</u>

Xenus are a ground squirrel that lives in South Africa.

They only weigh 1 to 2 pounds.

 **Y** is for a yellow-billed stork.

Derek Keats © <u>Wikimedia Commons</u>

They have a black tail, which shines with colors of green and purple.

The yellow-billed stork lives in Africa and Madagascar.

Z is for a zebra.

The zebra is cousins with donkeys and horses.

Zebras have stripes that help camouflage them in the tall grasses where they live.

Download Free Books!

http://MendonCottageBooks.com

Our books are available at

1. Amazon.com

2. Barnes and Noble

3. Itunes

4. Kobo

5. Smashwords

6. Google Play Books

Download Free Books!
http://MendonCottageBooks.com

Publisher

JD-Biz Corp

P O Box 374

Mendon, Utah 84325

http://www.jd-biz.com/

www.ingramcontent.com/pod-product-compliance
Lightning Source LLC
Chambersburg PA
CBHW050908290526
45792CB00002B/737